NATIONAL GEOGRAPHIC
OUR WORLD

My Day

by Emiliano Bermejo

T0349616

NATIONAL GEOGRAPHIC
LEARNING

I get up every morning. I have a shower.
Then I get dressed. Do you do that, too?

I don't get dressed, but I do have a shower. I make my own shower!

3

I eat breakfast every morning.
I like cereal for breakfast.
Do you like cereal, too?

I don't like cereal. I like insects.
I eat insects for breakfast!

5

Every afternoon, I play with my friends after school. Do you?

Every night, I eat dinner with my family.
Then I always do my homework.
After homework, I relax with my family.

I eat with my family at night,
but I don't do any homework!
I relax with my family, too.

After I do my homework, I brush my teeth. Then I go to bed. Do you go to bed at night?

I never go to bed at night!
I am awake all night.
I sleep all day.

Facts About Animals

Daytime Animals

Some animals are awake during the day.
They eat and do other things in the daylight.
These animals are called **diurnal animals**.

bald eagle

honeybee

meerkat

orangutans

Nighttime Animals

Other animals are awake at night. They eat and move around in the dark. These animals are called **nocturnal animals**.

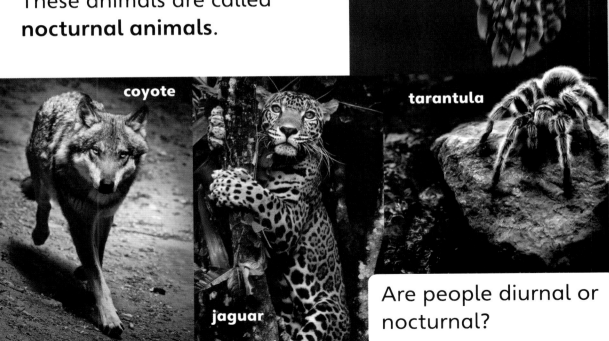

owl

coyote

jaguar

tarantula

Are people diurnal or nocturnal?

Fun with Daily Activities

What happens at each time of day? Write.

have breakfast   get up   have dinner   go to school   go to bed

6:45 A.M.

get up
_____

7:00 A.M.

_____

8:00 A.M.

_____

6:00 P.M.

_____

8:00 P.M.

_____

When do you usually do these things?
Circle the answer.

play with friends

(**afternoon**) night

brush my teeth

morning **afternoon**

do my homework

morning **night**

get dressed

morning **afternoon**

Glossary

awake

have/eat breakfast

have/eat dinner

insects

night

relax